500 FUNNY QUOTES FOR WOMEN

*Inspirational Quotes to Boost Your Mood Instantly
& Make Your Day A Little Happier!*

Edited by Stan Hardy

Notice:

Please note that the information contained within this document is for entertainment purposes only. All effort has been made to present accurate and reliable information. The content within this book has been derived from various sources. By reading this document, the reader agrees that under no circumstances is the author responsible for any losses, direct or indirect, which are incurred as a result of the use of the information contained within this document, including, but not limited to, errors, omissions, or inaccuracies.

TABLE OF CONTENTS

PREFACE

Humor sticks the most with people, especially when it is short and contains some truth or life lessons. That is why funny quotes are so great! They allow us to take a quick break, relax, and take life a bit easier. We can also draw inspiration from them, knowing that Albert Einstein, Ernest Hemingway, Charlie Chaplin, or some other great minds had the same experiences and struggles as ours.

This uplifting book provides 500 funny quotes with some of the universal truisms that are part of our everyday lives. The spectrum of quotes is as diverse as they are funny. Whether it is a quote about Relationships, Children, Age, Sports, Fun, People, or Religion, reading these can't help but make one smile, think, learn from their wisdom, chuckle, and refresh.

You can enjoy this book by reading it cover to cover or by going directly to your topic of interest. The quotes are carefully selected from various sources and thousands of quotes. All efforts have been made to check the quotes' source and to use the correct attributions. If you are looking for some quality, inspirational, and funny quotes to brighten your day, this is the book for you! If this book made you smile, please take the time to leave a review to help future readers like yourself and help me as a publisher. You might as well enjoy my other work with 500 funny quotes for men.

Thank you for your time. I hope you will have lots of fun!

Stan Hardy

Other Books by Dream Books LLC

"500 Funny Quotes For Men"

https://www.amazon.com/dp/B091G2SMPB

"Get It Done!: Beat Procrastination and Achieve Better Work-Life Balance!"

https://www.amazon.com/dp/B091G54S8P

MEN, WOMEN & RELATIONSHIPS

Men marry women with the hope they will never change. Women marry men with the hope they will change. Invariably they are both disappointed.

Albert Einstein

I love being married. It's so great to find that one special person you want to annoy for the rest of your life.

Rita Rudner

We sleep in separate rooms, we have dinner apart, we take separate vacations – we're doing everything we can to keep our marriage together.

Rodney Dangerfield

Not sure which is harder on a relationship: sharing a dresser for three years or sharing an iPhone charger for one day.

Rhea Butcher

The useless piece of flesh at the end of a penis is called a man.

Jo Brand

One should always be in love. That is the reason one should never marry.

Oscar Wilde

I do not want people to be very agreeable, as it saves me the trouble of liking them a great deal.

Jane Austen

Never follow anyone else's path. Unless you're in the woods and you're lost and you see a path. Then by all means follow that path.

Ellen DeGeneres

Men are like shoes. Some fit better than others. And sometimes you go out shopping and there's nothing you like. And then, as luck would have it, the next week you find two that are perfect, but you don't have the money to buy both.

Janet Evanovich

I hate women because they always know where things are.

Voltaire

Never trust a man with testicles.

Jo Brand

I've come to learn that the best time to debate family members is when they have food in their mouths.

Kenneth Cole, fashion designer

I like the male body; it's better designed than the male mind.

Andrea Newman

Women have more imagination than men. They need it to tell us how wonderful we are.

Arnold H. Glasow

Diamonds never leave you – men do!

Shirley Bassey

A successful man is one who makes more money than his wife can spend. A successful woman is one who can find such a man.

Lana Turner

Women are wiser than men because they know less and understand more.

James Thurber

My father always said, 'Never trust anyone whose TV is bigger than their bookshelf.'

Emilia Clarke

Most of us women like men, you know; it's just that we find them a constant disappointment.

Clare Short

Being a woman is a terribly difficult task since it consists principally in dealing with men.

Joseph Conrad

Women give us solace, but if it were not for women we would never need solace.

Don Herold

Women can talk, empathize, apply lipstick, see things using the eyes in the back of their head, remember birthdays, write lists, run the country and bark demands, all while executing a spot of parallel parking.

Liz Jones

My feeling is that women will never be equal to men. I think men are catching up in all kinds of ways.

Jack Dee

Only fine cigars are worth smoking and only men who smoke fine cigars are worth kissing.

Joan Collins

Men think about women. Women think about what men think about them.

Peter Ustinov

We women talk too much, but even then we don't tell half what we know.

Nancy Astor

Men don't know much about women. We do know when they're happy. We know when they're crying, and we know when they're pissed off. We just don't know in what order these are gonna' come at us.

Evan Davies

When a man opens a car door for his wife, it's either a new car or a new wife.

Prince Philip

American husbands are the best in the world; no other husbands are so generous to their wives, or can be so easily divorced.

Elinor Glyn

Love is just a system for getting someone to call you darling after sex.

Julian Barnes

Men always want to be a woman's first love – women like to be a man's last romance.

Oscar Wilde

I have never met anybody who has been made as happy by love as he has been made sad.

Alice Thomas Ellis

I saw six men kicking and punching the mother-in-law. My neighbor said, "Are you going to help?" I said, "No, six should be enough."

Les Dawson

Love is staying awake all night with a sick child. Or a very healthy adult.

David Frost

Do you seriously expect me to be the first Prince of Wales in history not to have a mistress?

Prince Charles

When my mother-in-law was born, they fired 21 guns. The only trouble was, they all missed.

Les Dawson

My friend spent £50 on a baby alarm and still got pregnant.

Linda Smith

Now the whole dizzying and delirious range of sexual possibilities has been boiled down to that one big, boring, bulimic word "*relationship*".

Julie Burchill

After eight years with my girlfriend she still gets annoyed if I use her toothbrush. Well, if she can tell me a better way of getting dog shit off my trainers.

Jimmy Carr

Powerful men often succeed through the help of their wives. Powerful women only succeed in spite of their husbands.

Linda Lee-Potter

Changeable women are more endurable than monotonous ones; they are sometimes murdered but rarely deserted.

George Bernard Shaw

My wife said to me, "If you won the lottery, would you still love me?" I said, "Of course I would. I'd miss you, but I'd still love you."

Frank Carson

I hate those ads for air fresheners: they are always populated by women and children, when we all know it is men who make the most smells.

Liz Jones

The war between the sexes is the only one in which both sides regularly sleep with the enemy.

Quentin Crisp

Talk to a woman as if you loved her, and talk to a man as if he bored you.

Oscar Wilde

Men, my dear, are very queer animals – a mixture of horse-nervousness, ass-stubbornness and camel-malice.

Thomas Henry Huxley

British men take you to McDonald's, make you pay and ask if anyone is dating your sister.

Minnie Driver

If I had to choose between him and a cockroach as a companion for a walking tour, the cockroach would have had it by a short head.

P.G. Wodehouse

Mr. Richard Harvey is going to be married, but as it is a great secret and only known to half of the neighborhood, you must not mention it.

Jane Austen

A dentist got married to a manicurist. They fought tooth and nail.

Tommy Cooper

A Royal Engineer serving overseas, wrote 200 love letters a week to his girlfriend back home. This Saturday, at All Saints Church, she marries the postman.

The Weekly Gazette

The only people I care to be very intimate with are the ones you feel would make a good third if God asked you out to dinner.

Nancy Mitford

That's it! I've had enough of men. There isn't one worth shaving your legs for. I'm going back to being a virgin.

Rose, Keeping Up Appearances

At the moment, I am debarred from the pleasure of putting her in her place by the fact that she has not got one.

Edith Sitwell

Love: a mutual misunderstanding

Oscar Wilde

Love is an ocean of emotions entirely surrounded by expenses.

Lord Dewar

The English really aren't interested in talking to you unless you've been to school or to bed with them.

Lady Nancy Keith

A man is two people, himself and his cock. A man always takes his friend to the party. Of the two, the friend is the nicer, being more able to show his feelings.

Beryl Bainbridge

Why are women so much more interesting to men than men are to women?

Virginia Woolf

I never married because there was no need. I have three pets at home which answer the same purpose as a husband. I have a dog which growls every morning, a parrot which swears all afternoon, and a cat that comes home late at night.

Marie Corelli

What every woman knows and no man can ever grasp is that even if he brings home everything on the list, he will still not have got the right things.

Allison Pearson

Talk to a man about himself and he will listen for hours.

Benjamin Disraeli

No one listened to one unless one said the wrong thing.

Sylvia Townsend Warner

We were married for better or worse. I couldn't have done better, and she couldn't have done worse.

Henny Youngman

When a man brings his wife flowers for no reason, there's a reason.

Molly McGee

A true friend stabs you in the front.

Oscar Wilde

It's a dilemma to not only have to choose what outfit to wear but which boyfriend to wear it with.

Tara Palmer-Tomkinson

It goes far towards reconciling me to being a woman when I reflect that I am thus in no danger of marrying one.

Lady Mary Wortley Montagu

She sat listening to the speech with the stoical indifference with which an Eskimo might accept the occurrence of a snowstorm the more, in the course of an Arctic winter.

Saki

Women, without her man, is nothing.

Women: without her, man is nothing.

Statement showing the importance of punctuation

There is only one thing in the world worse than being talked about, and that is not being talked about.

Oscar Wilde

Gossip is when you hear something you like about someone you don't.

Jane Seabrook

We always hold hands. If I let go, she shops.

Henny Youngman

I never knew how exciting dating could be until I got married.

Melanie White

Love is sharing your popcorn.

Charles Schultz

Love; A temporary insanity curable by marriage.

Ambrose Bierce

As a man in a relationship, you have a choice: You can be right or you can be happy.

Ralphie May

❧

What's the best way to have your husband remember your anniversary? Get married on his birthday.

Cindy Garner

❧

An archaeologist is the best husband any woman can have; the older she gets, the more interested he is in her.

Agatha Christie

❧

Whatever you may look like, marry a man your own age - as your beauty fades, so will his eyesight.

Phyllis Diller

❧

Spend a few minutes a day really listening to your spouse. No matter how stupid his problems sound to you.

Megan Mullally

❧

Marrying a man is like buying something you've been admiring for a long time in a shop window. You may love it when you get it home, but it doesn't always go with everything else.

Jean Kerr

The secret of a happy marriage remains a secret.

Henny Youngman

A successful relationship requires falling in love many times, always with the same person.

Mignon McLaughlin

Gravitation is not responsible for people falling in love.

Albert Einstein

Men are far more romantic than women. Men are the ones who'll say, "I've found somebody. She's amazing. If I don't get to be with this person, I can't carry on. If I'm not with her I'll end up in a bedsit, I'll be an alcoholic." That's how women feel about shoes.

Dylan Moran

18

Why buy a book when you can join the library?

Lily Savage, on marriage

I never feel more alone than when I'm trying to put sunscreen on my back.

Jimmy Kimmel

Instead of getting married again, I'm going to find a woman I don't like and just give her a house.

Rod Stewart, rock star

I think it should be like dog licenses. I think you should have to renew your marriage licenses every five years.

John Cleese

Marriage is a sort of friendship recognized by the police.

Robert Louis Stevenson

FRIENDSHIP

Friendship is not possible between two women, one of whom is very well dressed.

Laurie Colwin

There is nothing better than a friend unless it is a friend with chocolate.

Linda Grayson

One sure way to lose another woman's friendship is to try to improve her flower arrangements.

Marcelene Cox

A good friend will help you move. But a best friend will help you move a dead body.

Jim Hayes

A friend is someone who knows all about you and still loves you.

Elbert Hubbard

When you're in jail, a good friend will be trying to bail you out. A best friend will be in the cell next to you saying, Damn, that was fun.

Groucho Marx

Some people go to priests; others to poetry; I to my friends.

Virginia Woolf

Most of us don't need a psychiatric therapist as much as a friend to be silly with.

Robert Brault

Men kick friendship around like a football and it doesn't seem to crack. Women treat it like glass and it falls to pieces.

Anne Lindbergh

The holy passion of friendship is so sweet and steady and loyal and enduring a nature that it will last through a whole lifetime, if not asked to lend money.

Mark Twain

22

CHILDREN

The main purpose of children's parties is to remind you that there are children more awful than your own.

Katherine Whitehorn

When your children are teenagers, it's important to have a dog so that someone in the house is happy to see you.

Nora Ephron

I'm very hairy on my body and my wife is very ginger. We could very easily have an orang-utan.

Mike Gunn

Cleaning up with children around is like shoveling during a blizzard.

Margaret Culkin Banning

Before I got married, I had six theories about bringing up children; now I have six children and no theories.

John Wilmot

We spend the first twelve months of our children's lives teaching them to walk and talk and the next twelve telling them to sit down and shut up.

Phyllis Diller

Sometimes I am amazed that my wife and I created two human beings from scratch yet struggle to assemble the most basic of IKEA cabinets.

Malcolm Prince

They say men can never experience the pain of childbirth. They can if you hit them in the goolies with a cricket bat for fourteen hours.

Jo Brand

Adults are just children who earn money.

Kenneth Branagh

I asked my brother-in-law, the father of four boys, 'If you had it to do all over again, would you still have kids?' 'Yes,' he said. 'Just not these four.'

Sheila Lee

Youth is such a wonderful thing. What a crime to waste it on children.

George Bernard Shaw

I once bought my kids a set of batteries for Christmas with a note on it, saying, "Toys not included".

Bernard Manning

A lot of mothers will do anything for their children, except let them be themselves.

Banksy

I'd like to smack smug parents who say, "Our three-year-old's reading *Harry Potter*." Well, my three-year-old's smearing his shit on the fridge door.

Jack Dee

I really think that girls are born in conversation. I think they just pop out of the womb going, "Are you my mother? Lovely to put a name to a face. You, nurse, weigh me. Get it over with; it's the best it's ever going to be. Seven pounds one? It's downhill from here.

Michael McIntyre

When childhood dies, its corpses are called adults.

Brian Aldiss

Parents should leave books lying around marked "Forbidden" if they want their children to read.

Doris Lessing

If men had to have babies, they would only ever have one each.

Princess Diana

I don't dislike babies, though I think very young ones rather disgusting.

Queen Victoria

We have lots of rows about the whole baby thing. I wanted to have a baby for about five years, but my wife wants to keep it forever.

Lee Mack

Bringing up children on your own is very difficult, even when there are two parents.

Virginia Bottomley

Insanity is hereditary – you get it from your children.

Sam Levenson

28

SEX

I wouldn't kidnap a man for sex, but I'm not saying I couldn't use someone to oil the mower.

Victoria Wood

Yesterday morning my wife asked me to make love to her in the kitchen. When I asked why, she said the egg timer had broken and she wanted a soft-boiled egg.

David Brinham

When the sun comes up, I have morals again.

Elizabeth Taylor

I don't find English men sexy. They're all queer or kinky. The last Pom I went to bed with said to me, "Let's pretend you're dead."

Germaine Greer

Susan, you are offering this man food and sex in the same place. If there's something to read in the loo he may never leave.

Sally Harper (Kate Isitt), Coupling

People today say you cannot be happy unless your sex life is happy. That makes about as much sense as saying you cannot be happy unless your golf life is happy.

Evelyn Waugh

I had a wet dream about you last night. I dreamed you got hit by a bus, and I pissed myself laughing.

Jack Dee

The total amount of undesired sex endured by women is probably greater in marriage than in prostitution.

Bertrand Russell

I said to my wife, "Was you faking it last night?" She said, "No, I really was asleep."

Ricky Grover

It's incredible what men will interpret as sexual: "Did you see the way she looked at me before she told me to fuck off?"

Dylan Moran

When I had my daughters, I had to have stitches. I did ask them to put a couple of extra ones in, as a special treat for me husband, really. He said it really improved things. He said before that it was like waving a stick in the Albert Hall.

Pauline Calf (a.k.a Steve Coogan)

Sex is like supermarkets – overrated. Just a lot of pushing and shoving and you still come out with very little at the end.

Shirley Valentine

Why should we take advice on sex from the Pope? If he knows anything about it, he shouldn't.

George Bernard Shaw

Sex, on the whole, was meant to be short, nasty and brutish. If what you want is cuddling, you should buy a puppy.

Julie Burchill

Sex was not a subject we discussed in our family. I didn't even realize I had a vagina. The loss of my virginity was a process so lengthy and so painful that I thought, Oh, I see, the man actually has to make the hole by pounding away with his penis.

Julie Walters

I've only slept with men I've been married to. How many women can make that claim?

Elizabeth Taylor

Ken is so tired his sperm are on crutches.

Emma Thompson, on ex-husband Kenneth Branagh

I've never ever had sex apart from that one time eight months ago but apart from that I'm a complete virgin.

Vicky Pollard, Little Britain

At the Army medical, the doctor said, "Take all your clothes off." I said, "Shouldn't you take me out to dinner first?"

Spike Milligan

It's an extraordinary way of bringing babies into the world. I don't know how God thought of it

Winston Churchill

Who is this Greek chap Clitoris they're talking about?

Lord Albermarle

My wife is a sex object – every time I ask for sex, she objects.

Les Dawson

34

Sport

If you want to understand the effect of weight on a horse, try running for a bus with nothing in your hands. Then try doing it with your hands full of shopping. Then think about doing that for four and a half miles.

Jenny Pitman

Have you ever thought about the person who designed the sports skirt? Somebody sat down, drew a fantasy and made it compulsory uniform. I can never watch Wimbledon without thinking of that man.

Inspector Morse

When male golfers wiggle their feet to get their stance right, they look exactly like cats preparing to pee.

Jilly Cooper

- How do you think golf could be improved?

- I always feel that the hole is too small.

Interviewer with Mark James

I don't know much about football. I know what a goal is, which is surely the main thing about football.

Victoria Beckham

FASHION & BEAUTY

The sense of being well-dressed gives a feeling of inward tranquility, which religion is powerless to bestow.

C.F. Forbes

How on earth did Gandhi manage to walk so far in flip-flops? I can't last ten minutes in mine.

Mrs. Merton

After forty, a woman has to choose between losing her figure or her face. My advice is to keep your face and stay sitting down.

Dame Barbara Cartland

She wore far too much rouge last night and not quite enough clothes. That is always a sign of despair in a woman.

Oscar Wilde

Beauty is the first present nature gives to a woman and the first it takes away.

Fay Weldon

❧

Nothing inspires cleanliness more than an unexpected guest.

Radhika Mundra

❧

I can never be a nudist. I could never decide what not to wear.

Jennifer Coombs

❧

They say leather is mainly for perverts. Don't know why. Think it's very practical, actually. I mean, you spill anything on it, and it just comes of. I suppose that could be why the perverts like it.

Charlotte Coleman

❧

One thing I've learned from Star Trek is that men are going to be wearing simple pullovers forever. I've also learned, not to my surprise, that women will continue to sport minis and plenty of décolletages whatever the stardate.

Bernard Hollowood

❧

The best-dressed woman is one whose clothes wouldn't look too strange in the country.

Hardy Amies

There is no cosmetic for beauty like happiness.

Lady Blessington

I love new clothes. If everyone could just wear new clothes every day, I reckon depression wouldn't exist anymore.

Sophie Kinsella

Nothing gives a brighter glow to the complexion or makes the eye of a beautiful woman sparkle so intensely as triumph over another.

Lady Caroline Lamb

- I'm lending Nancy Mitford my villa in France so she can finish a book.

- Oh, really. What's she reading?

Friend and Dame Edith Evans

I dress sexily – but not in an obvious way; sexy in a virginal way.

Victoria Beckham

It has been said that a pretty face is a passport. But it's not, it's a visa, and it runs out fast.

Julie Burchill

The problem with beauty is that it's like being born rich and getting poorer.

Joan Collins

I have a suspicion that the photos on seed packets are posed by professional flowers.

Denis Norden

Do you know a shop where they cut your hair properly? I keep on having my hair cut, but it keeps on growing again.

G. K. Chesterton

Let us be grateful to the mirror for revealing to us our appearance only.

Samuel Butler

Well, madam, have you looked in the mirror and seen the state of your nose? Boxing is my excuse. What's yours?

Henry Cooper to Baroness Summerskill

The reason there are so few female politicians is that it is too much trouble to put make-up on two faces.

Maureen Murphy

I lent my wife £1,000 to have for plastic surgery; now I can't get the money back and I don't know who to look for.

Jethro (a.k.a. Geoff Rowe)

I wish I was covered in fur . . . or feathers . . . or something more interesting than just fat.

John Peel

Fashion is a form of ugliness so intolerable that we have to alter it every six months.

Oscar Wilde

The buttocks are the most aesthetically pleasing part of the body because they are non-functional. Although they conceal an essential orifice, these pointless globes are as near as the human form can ever come to abstract art.

Kenneth Tynan

My face is like five miles of bad country road.

Richard Harris

ART & CULTURE

All this modern art looks like bollocks so it must be worth something.

Edina Monsoon

Frankenstein is a book about what happens when a man tries to have a baby without a woman.

Anne K. Mellor

The difference between fiction and reality? Fiction has to make sense.

Tom Clancy, author

You should always believe what you read in newspapers, for that makes them more interesting.

Rose Macaulay

I told my mother I wanted to grow up and be a comedian. She said you can't do both.

Jimmy Carr

No good opera plot can be sensible, for people do not sing when they are feeling sensible.

W.H. Auden

An ambulance chasing a fire engine round a roundabout.

Dylan Moran, on dance music

All you have to do is to look like crap on film, and everyone thinks you're a brilliant actress. Actually, all you've done is look like crap.

Helen Mirren

My dad said, "Laughter is the best medicine," which is why, when I was six, I nearly died of diphtheria: "Dad, I can't breathe!" "Knock, knock . . ."

Dave Spikey

Television is for appearing on, not looking at.

Noel Coward

❦

She has the smile of a woman who has just dined off her husband.

Lawrence Durrell, on the Mona Lisa

❦

Every portrait that is painted with feeling is a portrait of the artist, not of the sitter.

Oscar Wilde

❦

Ladies, just a little more virginity, if you don't mind.

Herbert Beertbohm Tree

❦

The sound of laughter is the most civilized music in the world.

Peter Ustinov

❦

Orlando Bloom sounds like the love-child of Virginia Woolf and James Joyce.

Quentin Cooper

❦

Television is as injurious to the soul as fast food is to the body.

Quentin Crisp

A bad experience of Shakespeare is like a bad oyster – it puts you off for life.

Judi Dench

The length of a film should be directly related to the endurance of the human bladder.

Alfred Hitchcock

I love acting. It is so much more real than life.

Oscar Wilde

Bach almost persuades me to be a Christian.

Virginia Woolf

Bells are music's laughter.

Thomas Hood

They say an actor is only as good as his parts. Well, my parts have done me pretty well, darling.

Barbara Windsor

Sometimes people confuse me with Anthony Hopkins. Here's how you tell the difference: I'm the one nailing Mrs. Hopkins.

Michael Caine

If Peter O'Toole were any prettier, you'd have to call the film *Florence of Arabia.*

Noel Coward

Sometimes an orgasm is better than being on the stage. Sometimes being on the stage is better than an orgasm.

Mick Jagger

Comedy is the one job you can do badly and no one will laugh at you.

Max Miller

Two people writing a novel is like three people having a baby.

Evelyn Waugh

The finest collection of frames I ever saw.

Sir Humphry Davy on the Paris art galleries

Agatha Christie has given more pleasure in bed than any other woman.

Nancy Banks-Smith

- Two tickets reserved for you for the first night of my new play. Bring a friend. If you have one.

- Cannot make the first night. Will come the second night. If you have one.

George Bernard Shaw and Winston Churchill

There are two motives for reading a book: one, that you enjoy it; the other, that you can boast about it.

Bertrand Russell

Literature is the art of writing something that will be read twice; journalism what will be grasped at once.

Cyril Connolly

50

HOBBIES & FUN

Recreation: hunting, fishing, shooting, food, rugby, men.

Clarissa Dickson Wright

The British are not good at having fun. I get overexcited if there's a pattern on my kitchen roll.

Victoria Wood

You can't get a cup of tea big enough or a book long enough to suit me.

C.S. Lewis

You know what really pisses me off? When you're on a plane, and the hostess comes up to you and asks you to stop singing. Hold on, you've been giving me free drinks for five hours – what do you expect me to do?

Sean Lock

For men, shopping is like sex. They can only manage it for five minutes and then they get tired.

Jeff Green

❧

I went window shopping today. I bought four windows.

Tommy Cooper

❧

At the age of 80, there are very few pleasures left to me, but one of them is passive smoking.

Baroness Trumpington

❧

One half of the world cannot understand the pleasure of the other.

Jane Austen

❧

To truly laugh, you must be able to take your pain, and play with it.

Charlie Chaplin

❧

Happiness is the perpetual possession of being well deceived.

Lytton Strachey

Some cause happiness wherever they go; others, whenever they go.

Oscar Wilde

The only way of preventing civilized men from beating and kicking their wives is to organize games in which they can kick and beat balls.

George Bernard Shaw

Let's face it; football is a game of the commoners. As soon as you get a mortgage, you start liking tennis.

Jonathan Ross

Bad humor is an evasion of reality; good humor is an acceptance of it.

Malcolm Muggeridge

To relax, I put Smarties tubes on cats' legs to make them walk like a robot. If I'm really in the mood for fun, I make them walk downstairs.

Jimmy Carr

Imagination was given to man to compensate him for what he is not, a sense of humor to console him for what he is.

Francis Bacon, philosopher

I remember once having to stop performing when I thought an elderly man a few rows back from the front was actually going to die because he was laughing so hard.

Adrian Edmondson

In 1969 I gave up drinking and sex. It was the worst twenty minutes of my life.

George Best

- So, you got drunk again last night. Why was that?

- Because I was sober.

Ardal O'Hanlon

KNOWLEDGE & EDUCATION

Lack of education is an extraordinary handicap when one is being offensive.

Josephine Tay

The first time you leave your child at school you're faced with a tough decision – down the pub or back to bed?

Jo Brand

I spend all my time arguing with the spell-check on my computer.

Ann Widdecombe

He is the intellectual without the intellect.

John McKenna

56

I chose a single-sex Oxford college because I thought I'd rather not face the trauma of men at breakfast.

Theresa May

I am patient with stupidity but not with those who are proud of it.

Edith Sitwell

The greatest life lesson is to know that even fools are sometimes right.

Winston Churchill

Originality is undetected plagiarism.

Dean Inge

Nothing that is worth knowing could be taught.

Oscar Wilde

To know all is not to forgive all. It is to despise everybody.

Quentin Crisp

I'd always thought her half-baked, but now I think they didn't even put her in the oven.

P.G. Wodehouse

A great many of people think they are thinking when they are merely rearranging their prejudices.

William James

If there was graffiti in a lavatory cubicle, I had to read every word and sometimes even corrected the spelling and punctuation.

Sue Townsend

This is the sort of English up with which I will not put.

Winston Churchill

The trouble with words is that you never know whose mouth they've been in.

Dennis Potter

The only time my education was interrupted was when I was at school.

George Bernard Shaw

Men are born ignorant, not stupid. They are made stupid by education.

Bertrand Russell

My school report said that I was every inch a fool. Fortunately, I was not very tall.

Sir Norman Wisdom

LUCK & HAPPINESS

The British do not expect happiness. I had the impression, all the time that I lived there, that they did not want to be happy; they want to be right.

Quentin Crisp

A large income is the best recipe for happiness I ever heard of.

Jane Austen

The insurance man told me that the accident policy covered falling off the roof but not hitting the ground.

Tommy Cooper

If you want to be happy for a short time, get drunk; happy for a long time, fall in love; happy forever, take up gardening.

Arthur Smith

All the things I like to do are either immoral, illegal, or fattening.

Alexander Woollcott, actor

Good friends, good books, and a sleepy conscience: this is the ideal life.

Mark Twain

A Short message from the Editor

Hey, hope you're enjoying the book. I'd love to hear your thoughts!

Many readers do not know how hard reviews are to come by, and how much they help an author.

I would be incredibly thankful if you could take just 60 seconds to write a brief review on Amazon, even if it's just a few sentences!

>> Click here to leave a quick review

Thank you for taking the time to share your thoughts!

Your review will genuinely make a difference for me and help gain exposure for my work.

FOOD & DRINK

English coffee tastes the way a long-standing family joke sounds when you try to explain it to outsiders.

Margaret Halsey

If you want to confuse a girl, buy her a pair of chocolate shoes.

Milton Jones

Pratchett's guide to mushrooms: One: All fungi are edible. Two: Some fungi are not edible more than once.

Terry Pratchett

Never drink black coffee at lunch; it will keep you awake all afternoon.

Jilly Cooper

Triangular sandwiches taste better than square ones.

Peter Kay

❦

Stop being a vegan and start enjoying what you eat.

Jamie Oliver

❦

They say cheese gives you nightmares. Ridiculous! I'm not scared of cheese!

Ross Noble

❦

Why does mineral water that "has trickled through mountains for centuries" have a "use-by" date?

Peter Kay

❦

If the British can survive their meals, they can survive anything.

George Bernard Shaw

❦

CHARACTER & MANNERS

Even crushed against his brother in the Tube, the average Englishman pretends desperately that he is alone.

Germaine Greer

Manners are especially the need of the plain. The pretty can get away with anything.

Evelyn Waugh

Depression is the most extreme form of vanity.

Julie Burchill

My kids have beautiful manners. Our Jason may be a car thief, but he always leaves a thank-you note on the pavement.

Lily Savage

66

She never lets ideas interrupt the easy flow of her conversation.

Jean Webster, author

- I will not fuck it up again, Mum.

- Bridget! Language!

- Sorry. I will not fuck it up again, Mother.

Bridget Jones and Mum, Bridget Jones – The Edge of Reason

I am all in favor of spontaneity, providing it is carefully planned and ruthlessly controlled.

John Gielgud

If there's one thing I can't stand it's snobbism. People who pretend they're superior make it so much harder for those of us who really are.

Haycinth Bucket, Keeping Up Appearances

He ought to run a hospital for sick jokes.

Anthony Powell

Angels can fly because they take things lightly.

G. K. Chesterton

Last time I went on an Intercity train there were a couple across the aisle having sex. Of course, this being a British train, nobody said anything. Then they finished, they both lit up a cigarette and this woman stood up and said, "Excuse me, I think you'll find this is a non-smoking compartment."

Victoria Wood

Be wiser than other people, if you can, but do not tell them so.

Lord Chesterfield

It seldom pays to be rude. It never pays to be half-rude.

Norman Douglas

A gentleman is one who can fold a newspaper in a crowded train.

Leonora Cunningham

Silence is the correct answer to an unasked question.

Armando Iannucci

My wife loves the c-word. Sometimes, when the children are listening, she combines it with "bastard" to create "custard".

Jeremy Clarkson

The mechanic said that if it had been a horse, he'd have had to shoot her.

Basil Boothroyd

After a taxi ride, Tommy Cooper would slip something into the top pocket of the driver and say, "Have a drink on me." When the taxi driver looked in his pocket, he'd find it was a teabag.

Bob Monkhouse

Could you ask our captain to go a little faster and land a little earlier? My husband would tip him handsomely.

Hyacinth Bucket, at the check-in desk, Keeping Up Appearances

I looked up some of the symptoms of pregnancy: moody, irritable, big bosoms. I've obviously been pregnant for 36 years.

Victoria Wood

I believe in the discipline of silence and could talk for hours about it.

George Bernard Shaw

If you apologize for turning your back, the Chinese reply, "A rose has no back."

Geoffrey Madan

A little nonsense now and then is cherished by the wisest men.

Roald Dahl

If you believe that your thoughts originate inside your brain, do you also believe that television shows are made inside your television set?

Warren Ellis

I still like a man to open a door for me – even if he does let it swing back and hit me in the face.

Pauline Daniels

I love children – especially when they cry, for then someone takes them away.

Nancy Mitford

My New Year's resolution is to refrain from saying witty, unkind things unless they are really witty and irreparably damaging.

James Agate

Intuition is the strange instinct that tells a woman she is right, whether she is or not.

Oscar Wilde

During an outing on a safari trip to Africa with a group of fellow British tourists, a friend of mine stopped for a pee. Having located a suitable bush, she relieved herself but was amazed at standing up to find a queue of ladies behind her all waiting for the same bush.

Catherine Betts

This is the only country in the world where you step on somebody's foot, and he apologizes.

Keith Waterhous on England

If you can't be a good example, then you'll just have to serve as a horrible warning.

Catherine Aird

A man who moralizes is usually a hypocrite, and a woman who moralizes is invariably plain.

Oscar Wilde

The lie is the basic building block of good manners. That may seem mildly shocking to a moralist – but then what isn't?

Quentin Crisp

His courtesy was somewhat extravagant. He would write and thank the people who wrote to thank him for wedding presents, and when he encountered anyone as punctilious as himself, the correspondence ended only with death.

Evelyn Waugh

First things first, but not necessarily in that order.

Dr. Who

Ghosts, like ladies, never speak till spoke to.

Richard Harris Braham

I could not fail to disagree with you less.

Boris Johnson

There are some people who suddenly get loads of money who become very tasteless. How have you two managed to avoid that?

Ali G (a.k.a. Sacha Baron Cohen), interviewing David and Victoria Beckham for Comic Relief

Manners are the outward expression of expert interior decoration.

Noel Coward

My father and he had one of those English friendships which begin by avoiding intimacies and eventually eliminate speech altogether.

Jorge Luis Borges

The English never speak to anyone unless they have been properly introduced (except in case of shipwreck).

Pierre Daninos

A gentleman never eats. He breakfasts, he lunches, he dines, but he never eats.

Lord Fotherham

The more the English dislike you, the more polite they are.

Rabbi Lionel Blue

74

Class & Royalty

Middle-class girls get degrees. The working class get jobs. And the underclass get a baby as soon as they can.

Tony Parsons

It was lovely to talk to the Queen, especially since I am a Windsor too.

Barbara Windsor

Never keep up with the Joneses. Drag them down to your level. It's cheaper.

Quentin Crisp

Oh, I do hope you're not going to spoil everything with lower-middle-class humor.

Hyacinth Bucket, Keeping Up Appearances

Prince Andrew and Sarah met on the polo field, doesn't everybody?

Susan Barrantes, mother of Sarah Fergusen

Buckingham Palace rejected a suggestion by Mrs. Thatcher that a procedure be instituted to ensure she and the Queen never appear in public in similar or identical outfits with this terse reply: "Her Majesty never notices what anyone wears."

Laura Grey

Isn't it amazing that Camilla looks exactly like Princess Diana if she had survived the car crash?

Frankie Boyle

How low and unbecoming a thing laughing is: not to mention the disagreeable noise that it makes and the shocking distortion of the face.

Lord Chesterfield

The trouble with being a princess is that it's so hard to have a pee.

Princess Diana

The post is hopeless, and I have given up sending things by post. I have things delivered in my Rolls Royce.

Barbara Cartland

How shall we ever know if it's morning if there's no servant to pull up the blind?

J.M. Barrie, The Admirable Crichton

Gentlemen are requested, and servants are commanded to keep off the grass.

Sign in London park, 19th century

"How wonderful it must have been for the Ancient Britons," my mother said once, "when the Romans arrived, and they could have a Hot Bath."

Katharine Whitehorn

HEALTH

- How are you feeling?

- I'm dying but otherwise, I'm in perfect health.

Friend and Edith Sitwell

When I was a nurse, my favorite assignment was the anorexic ward. Sometimes I ate as many as 17 dinners.

Jo Brand

Lord Dawson was not a good doctor. King George V told me that he would not have died, had he had another doctor.

Margot Asquith

Be careful about reading health books. You may die of a misprint.

Mark Twain

Free your mind, and your bottom will follow.

Sarah Ferguson

I've got my figure back after giving birth. Sad, I'd hope to get somebody else's.

Caroline Quentin

I asked my doctor for something for persistent wind. He gave me a kite.

Les Dawson

Wine; a constant proof that God loves us and loves to see us happy.

Benjamin Franklin

FOOD & DIET

I would walk miles for a bacon sandwich.

Diana, Princess of Wales

I'm in shape. Round is a shape.

George Carlin

Don't dig your grave with your knife and fork.

English proverb.

Things taste better in small houses.

Queen Victoria

I found out there was only one way to look thin: hang out with fat people.

Rodney Dangerfield

I love the philosophy of a sandwich. It typifies my attitude to life. It's all there, it's fun, it looks good, and you don't have to wash up afterwards.

Molly Parkin

A woman should never be seen eating or drinking, unless it be lobster, salad and champagne, the only truly feminine viands.

Lord Byron

Tourists tend to enjoy the traditional English breakfast because they don't eat such things often at home. If they did, they would die.

Lonely Planet guide to Britain

Diets are like boyfriends – it never really works to go back to them.

Nigella Lawson

The name Big Mac is generally supposed to have come about because it is a big McDonald's burger, but in fact, it was named after a big raincoat whose taste resembles.

Joe Brand

The Englishman who visits Mount Etna will carry his tea kettle to the top.

Ralph Waldo Emerson

I just love Chinese food. My favorite dish is number twenty-seven.

Clement Attlee

ANIMALS

I dislike monkeys: they always remind me of my poor relations.

Henry Lutrell

A dog is not intelligent. Never trust an animal that's surprised by its own farts.

Frank Skinner

Why didn't evolution give them genes to make them good at carpentry, then, so they could build a ladder instead of growing long necks?

Karl Pilkington, on giraffes

If God did not intend for us to eat animals, then why did he make them out of meat?

John Cleese

A dog teaches a boy fidelity, perseverance, and to turn around three times before lying down.

Robert Benchley, humorist

A man loses his dog so he puts an ad in the paper. And the ad says, "Here boy!"

Spike Milligan

Cats are smarter than dogs. You can't get eight cats to pull a sled through snow.

Jeff Valdez, producer

Did St. Francis preach to the birds? Whatever for? If he really liked birds, he would have done better to preach the cats.

Rebecca West

A bird in the hand invariably shits on your wrist.

Billy Connolly

Red squirrels . . . you don't see many of them since they became extinct.

Michael Aspel

Why do dogs always race to the door when the doorbell rings when it's hardly ever for them?

Harry Hill

The male gypsy moth can smell the female gypsy moth up to seven miles away – and that fact also works if you remove the word "moth".

Jimmy Carr

Dogs look up to you. Cats look down to you. Give me a pig. He just looks you in the eye and treats you as an equal.

Winston Churchill

Among the mammals, only man has ears that can display no emotion.

W. H. Auden

If you leave a dog locked in a car on a hot day, it will die in about half an hour. If you leave the heating on, you can get that down to about ten minutes.

Sean Meo

LIFE & DEATH

Life was planned by a committee while the clever ones had popped out to the lav.

Victoria Wood

If you don't know where you are going, any road will get you there.

Lewis Carroll

Men were born to lie, and women to believe them.

John Gay

Life's not fair, is it? Some of us drink champagne in the fast lane, and some of us eat our sandwiches by the loose chippings on the A597.

Victoria Wood

I have a nervous breakdown in the film, and in one scene, I get to stand at the top of the stairs waving an empty sherry bottle which is, of course, a typical scene from my daily life, so isn't much of a stretch.

Emma Thompson

I was taking my dog for a stroll in the cemetery early one day, and a woman passed me by and said, "Morning!" I said, "No, just walking the dog."

John Mann

If you live to be one hundred, you've got it made. Very few people die past that age.

George Burns

In Liverpool, the difference between a funeral and a wedding is one less drunk.

Paul O'Grady

The leading cause of death in this world is birth.

Mitch Murray

I wouldn't say my mother-in-law is fat, but when she was run over recently the driver said it was because he didn't have enough petrol to go around her.

Jimmy Tarbuck

- So. You're going to Parslow's funeral.

- Yes. Even though it's very unlikely that he'll ever come to mine.

Mrs. Blewitt and Arkwright, Open All Hours

I'm fascinated that hair grows after death; I'm looking forward to that.

Clive Anderson

Death is the last enemy: once we've got past that, I think everything will be all right.

Alice Thomas Ellis

Have you noticed that all the people in favor of birth control are already born?

Benny Hill

It's a good rule of life never to apologize. The right sort of people don't want apologies, and the wrong sort takes a mean advantage of them.

P. G. Wodehouse

Remember, if a man twists his wife, he will twist anyone else.

Norris McWhirter

Parents are the bones on which children sharpen their teeth.

Peter Ustinov

I don't know what I want, but I want it NOW!

Vivian Stanshall

For sale: Undertaker's overcoat. Slightly worn on one shoulder.

Loot Magazine

I blame myself for my boyfriend's death. I shot him.

Jo Brand

After being an awed witness of the funeral of King Edward VII, the little daughter of Lord Kinnoull refused to say her prayers that night: "God will be too busy unpacking King Edward," she said.

Lord Riddell

Well, thank you, Rector, it was a lovely funeral. We must have one again sometime.

Audrey Ffrobes-Hamilton, To The Manor Born

Should a father be present at the birth of his child? It's all any reasonable child can expect if dad is present at the conception.

Joe Orton

We cannot tear out a single page of our life, but we can throw the whole book in the fire.

George Eliot

I hope I go like my mother. She just sat up, broke wind, and died.

Ena Sharples, Coronation Street

The trouble with children is that they are not returnable.

Quentin Crisp

A French five minutes is ten minutes shorter than a Spanish five minutes but slightly longer than an English five minutes, which is usually ten minutes.

Guy Bellamy

For most people, death comes at the end of their lives.

Greater London radio presenter

Everyone seems to fear dying alone, and I have never understood this point of view. Who wants to have to die and be polite at the same time?

Quentin Crisp

Life is a tragedy when seen in close-up, but a comedy in long-shot.

Charlie Chaplin

When you've told someone that you've left them a legacy, the only decent thing to do is to die at once.

Samuel Butler

Dear World, I am leaving because I am bored. I feel I have lived long enough. I am leaving you with your worries in this sweet cesspool. Good luck.

George Sanders, Suicide note

There are many who dare not kill themselves for fear of what the neighbors will say.

Cyril Connolly

You live and learn. Then you die and forget it all.

Noel Coward

May you die in bed at 95, shot by a jealous spouse.

Irish blessing

96

While other people's deaths are deeply sad, one's own is surely a bit of a joke.

James Cameron

Crucifixion… it's a slow, horrible death. But at least it gets you out into the open.

Matthias, Monty Python's Life of Brian

I never made a mistake in my life. I thought I did once, but I was wrong.

Charles M. Schulz

Life is hard; it's harder if you're stupid.

John Wayne

Life is like a roll of toilet paper, hopefully long and useful, but it always ends at the wrong moment.

Rudyh

My life has no purpose, no direction, no aim, no meaning, and yet I'm happy. I can't figure it out. What am I doing right?

Charles Schulz

Life is funny; when you are young, you want to be older, and those that are older wish to be younger.

Karon Waddell

Life is so constructed that an event does not, cannot, will not, match the expectation.

Charlotte Bronte

Life does not cease to be funny when people die any more than it ceases to be serious when people laugh.

George Bernard Shaw

Life is hard, after all, it kills you.

Kathrine Hepburn

We all pay for life with death, so everything in between should be free.

Bill Hicks

Embrace the glorious mess that you are.

Elizabeth Gilbert

Don't worry about the world coming to an end today. It's already tomorrow in Australia.

Charles M. Schulz

CRIME & PUNISHMENT

If you are ever attacked in the street, do not shout "Help!", shout "Fire!". People adore fires and always come rushing. Nobody will come if you shout "Help!".

Jean Trumpington

Sentence first, verdict afterwards.

Lewis Carroll, Alice's Adventures in Wonderland

Justice is being allowed to do whatever I like. Injustice is whatever prevents me doing it.

Samuel Butler

Crime is terribly revealing. Try and vary your methods as you will, your tastes, your habits, your attitude of mind, and your soul is revealed by your actions.

Agatha Christie

"Senseless" is a word usually applied to vandalism, but when one grasps the simple proposition that vandals obviously enjoy breaking things, the vandalism is no more senseless than playing tennis.

Auberon Waugh

Ma always told me she used to keep half a brick in her handbag, just in case.

Michael Bentine

A lawyer will do anything to win a case; sometimes, he will even tell the truth.

Patrick Murray

There is no satisfaction in hanging a man who does not object to it.

George Bernard Shaw

One wonders what would happen in a society in which there were no rules to break. Doubtless, everyone would quickly die of boredom.

Susan Howatch

AGE

People always live forever when there is any annuity to be paid to them.

Jane Austen

Middle age is when you look at the rain teeming down and say: "That'll be good for the garden."

Grace Marshall

The secret to staying young is to live honestly, eat slowly, and lie about your age.

Lucille Ball

Moisturizers do work. The rest is pap. There is nothing on God's earth that will take away 30 years of arguing with your husband.

Anita Roddick

Age is an issue of mind over matter. If you don't mind, it doesn't matter.

Mark Twain

How long a minute is, depends on which side of the bathroom door you're in.

Rob Monkhouse

I've found a way to make my wife drive more carefully. I told her that if she has an accident, the newspapers would print her age.

Jim Murray

A man's as old as he's feeling. A woman is as old as she looks.

Samuel Taylor Coleridge

As you get older, three things happen. The first is your memory goes, and I can't remember the other two . . .

Norman Wisdom

The old believe everything, the middle-aged suspect everything, the young know everything.

Oscar Wilde

There are three classes into which all the women past seventy that ever I knew were to be divided. One: That dear old soul; two: That old woman; three: That old witch.

Samuel Taylor Coleridge

RELIGION

I asked him why he was a priest, and he said if you have to work for anybody, an absentee boss is best.

Jeanette Winterson

I'm not a religious woman, but I find if you say no to everything, you can hardly tell the difference.

Mrs. Featherstone, Open All Hours

When I was in a convent in Belgium, I had to bathe in a bath which was sheeted over to prevent my guardian angel from seeing me.

Marie Tempest

The first time I sang in the church choir, two hundred people changed their religion.

Fred Allen

If Jesus was a Jew, how come he has a Mexican first name?

Billy Connolly

We were discussing the possibility of making one of our cats Pope recently, and we decided that the fact that she was not Italian, and she was female, made the third point, that she was a cat, quite irrelevant.

Katherine Whitehorn

My heaven will be filled with wonderful young men and dukes.

Barbara Cartland

One thing I shall miss in heaven is gardening. We shan't have weeds in heaven, shall we?

Catherine Bramwell-Booth

Two guys came knocking at my door once and said, "We want to talk to you about Jesus." I said, "Oh, no, what's he done now?"

Kevin McAleer

We know he [Jesus Christ] wasn't English because he wore sandals, but never with socks.

Linda Smith

My mother was worried about whether my father would be wearing pajamas or mackintosh in the afterlife.

George Melly

Prayers must not be answered: if it is, it ceases to be prayers and becomes correspondence.

Oscar Wilde

In the Bible: No one coughs. One person sneezes. Only one woman's age is mentioned (Sarah: 127).

Geoffrey Madan

Historically, more people have died of religion than of cancer.

Dick Francis

When I was a child, I used to think that the Day of Judgement meant that we were all going to judge God, and I still don't see why not.

Lord Berners

Men will wrangle for religion, write for it; fight for it; die for it; anything but live for it.

Charles Colton

I've come to view Jesus much the way I view Elvis. I love the guy, but the fan clubs really freak me out.

John Fugelsang

BUSINESS & MONEY

Never economize on luxuries.

Angela Thirkell

People who say money can't buy you happiness just don't know where to shop.

Tara Palmer Tomkinson

Imagine six apartments. It isn't so hard to do; one is full of fur coats, the others full of shoes

Elton John, 40th birthday card message to John Lennon

There are few sorrows, however poignant, in which a good income is of no avail.

L.P. Smith

Always suspect any job men willingly vacate for women.

Jill Tweedie

Sexual harassment at work. Is it a problem for the self-employed?

Victoria Wood

Lack of money is the root of all evil.

George Bernard Shaw

Saving is a very fine thing, especially when your parents have done it for you.

Winston Churchill

I yield to no one in my admiration for the office as a social center, but it's no place actually to get any work done.

Katherine Whitehorn

He was so mean, he only breathed in.

Bob Monkhouse

The salesman who sold me the car told me I'd get a lot of pleasure out of it. He was right. It was a pleasure to get out of it.

Les Dawson

Bankruptcy is like losing your virginity. It doesn't hurt the next time.

Clarissa Dickson-Wright

One of the symptoms of an approaching nervous breakdown is the belief that one's work is terribly important.

Bertrand Russell

They say a woman's work is never done. Maybe that's why they get paid less.

Sean Lock

Happy is the man with a wife to tell him what to do and a secretary to do it.

Lord Stormont Mancroft

The man with a toothache thinks everyone happy whose teeth are sound. The poverty-stricken man makes the same mistake about the rich man.

George Bernard Shaw

The value of money is that with it we can tell any man to go to the devil. It is the sixth sense which enables you to enjoy the other five.

W. Somerset Maugham

The amount of money some parents want to spend . . . would enable baby Jesus to leave the stable and check in to a five-star hotel.

Ed Watson, on nativity play costumes

I've just heard the best definition of English meanness. A friend has a weekend cottage in the country, with a bit of a garden. He hangs up bird feeders because he likes the sound and the flutter. Before he leaves on Sunday, he takes them down and puts them in the shed.

A.A. Gill

Multitasking is the ability to screw everything up simultaneously.

Jeremy Clarkson

- What is two and two?

- Are you buying or selling?

Small child and Lew Grade

The one phrase it is imperative to know in every foreign language is: my friend will pay.

Alan Whicker

Had an amazing cab driver. He was smiling and whistling – clearly in a brilliant mood. He said, "I love my job, I'm my own boss. Nobody tells me what to do." I said, "Left here."

Jimmy Carr

Half the money my company has spent on advertising was wasted. The problem is to find out which half.

Lord Leverhulme

I just realized that 'Let me check my calendar' is the adult version of 'Let me ask my mom.'

Noelle Chatham

Robin Hood is my hero. Have I robbed the rich and given the poor? Well, half of that.

Lee Hurst

Actually, I have no regard for money. Aside from its purchasing power, it's completely useless as far as I'm concerned.

Alfred Hitchcock

Victoria pointed to her necklace and said, "£1.5 million." David introduced himself. I was staring at his wife's tits and shouting. "How much?"

Graham Norton, on meeting David and Victoria Beckham

Economics is the systematic complication of the simple truths of housekeeping.

Philip Howard

The end... almost!

Reviews are not easy to come by. As an independent author with a tiny marketing budget, I rely on readers, like you, to leave a short review on Amazon. Even if it's just a sentence or two!

Customer reviews

☆☆☆☆☆ 963
5.0 out of 5 stars ▾

5 star		100%
4 star		0%
3 star		0%
2 star		0%
1 star		0%

See all 963 customer reviews ›

Share your thoughts with other customers

Write a customer review ⬅

So if you enjoyed the book, please...

>> Click here to leave a brief review on Amazon.

I am very appreciative for your review as it truly makes a difference. Many thanks for purchasing this book and reading it to the end!

116

MISCELLANEOUS

The best piece of advice I ever received was: "Don't do it again."

Lord Cudlipp

The only statistics you can trust are those you falsified yourself.

Winston Churchill

I have one golden rule: I ask myself what Nanny would have expected me to do.

Lord Carrington

Don't give a woman advice: one should never give a woman anything she can't wear in the evening.

Oscar Wilde

Experts have spent years developing weapons which can destroy people's lives but leave the buildings intact. They're called mortgages.

Jeremy Hardy

Housekeeping is like being caught in a revolving door.

Marcelene Cox

I was once paged at JFK airport as "Mr. No One."

Peter Noone

Never spit in a man's face unless his mustache is on fire.

Henry Root

I always tell a young man not to use the word "always".

Robert Walpole

History will be kind to me, for I intend to write it.

Winston Churchill

Maybe this world is another planet's hell.

Aldous Huxley

It is not so much that the world that's got so much worse, but news coverage that's go so much better.

G.K. Chesterton

For there was never yet philosopher

That could bear the toothache patiently.

William Shakespeare

I have tried in my time to be a philosopher, but cheerfulness always kept breaking in.

Oliver Edwards

All philosophies, if you ride them home, are nonsense; but some are greater nonsense than others.

Samuel Butler

If God had intended men to smoke, he'd have put chimneys in their heads.

J. B. Priestley

A good cigar is as great a comfort to a man as a good cry is to a woman.

Sir Edward Bulwer Lytton

- Name a major disease associated with smoking.

- Premature death.

GCSE exam answer

There are various ways to give up smoking – nicotine patches, nicotine gum. My auntie used to pour a gallon of petrol over herself every morning.

Paul Merton

My mum told me I'd better get a toilet brush, so I did. I've been using it for a week, but I think I'm going back to paper.

Dave Spikey

Give up smoking by sticking one cigarette from each new pack up a fat friend's arse, filter first, then replacing it in the box. The possibility of putting that one in your mouth will put off smoking any of them.

VIZ, Top tip

⁓

Madman are always serious; they go mad from lack of humor.

G.K. Chesterton

⁓

I didn't have a nervous breakdown. I was clinically fed up for two years.

Alan Partridge

⁓

The trouble with tranquilizers is that you find yourself being nice to the people you don't like.

Mark Bushman

⁓

The English climate: on a fine day, like looking up a chimney; on a rainy day, like looking down it.

Thomas Moore

⁓

Everybody talks about the weather, but nobody does anything about it.

Charles D. Warner

I have no relish for the country; it is a kind of a healthy grave.

Sydney Smith

Never join a queue unless you know what's at the end of it.

Gerald Challis

The trouble with retirement is that you never get a day off.

Abe Lemons

If you are going through hell, keep going.

Winston Churchill

Know thyself – but don't tell anyone.

H. F. Henrichs

Printed in Great Britain
by Amazon

41106428R00078